KU-020-145

"BARMBY MOOR C.E.
SCHOOL LIBRARY
PLEASE RETURN THIS BOOK
AS SOON AS POSSIBLE"

UNDERSTANDING RELIGIONS

Marriage Customs

Anita Compton

Wayland

Understanding Religions

Birth Customs
Death Customs
Food and Fasting
Initiation Customs
Marriage Customs
Pilgrimages and Journeys

About this book

This book looks at customs associated with marriage in different religious traditions around the world. It describes different ceremonies, and the significance of promises made and contracts signed by the couple who are getting married. The book shows that many rituals and symbols connected with marriage have their roots in basic principles about family life. Looking at various wedding celebrations can lead to an understanding of these fundamental beliefs.

Each chapter examines an aspect of marriage celebrations across the religions so that readers may compare customs and beliefs. The quotations in the book will encourage children to look at the religious practices of their own and others' communities. Teachers will find that elements of each chapter can be used as starting points for discussion and further study.

Editor: Joanna Housley
Designer: Malcolm Walker

First published in 1992 by
Wayland (Publishers) Limited
61 Western Road, Hove
East Sussex, BN3 1JD, England

© Copyright 1992 Wayland (Publishers) Limited

British Library Cataloguing in Publication Data
Compton, Anita
   Marriage Customs. (Understanding Religions Series)
   I. Title II. Series
   291.4

ISBN 0 7502 0420 6

Typeset by Kudos Editorial and Design Services
Printed in Italy by G Canale C.S.p.A. Turin

Contents

Words that appear in **bold** in the text are explained in the glossary on page 30.

Introduction

Can you become an unusual detective - a person who can recognize and describe customs? Can you also look behind the customs and ask why people do these things?

Customs

A custom is something that people do at special times and on special occasions in a family, a religion, a country, or a society. Customs mark events to remember. This book will explore certain marriage customs. Some will be ordinary, others

Below Couples who do not have arranged marriages go out together for some time to get to know each other before they get married.

Above A wedding is an occasion for families to come together. This Sikh couple are surrounded by members of their families, who join in the celebrations of their wedding day.

arc **sacred**, which means they carry hidden religious messages.

Some customs are linked to new beginnings: marriage is a new beginning for two people. A marriage is celebrated at a **ceremony** called a wedding. At a wedding there are various customs which show that the bride and groom are making an agreement to care for each other, and share the ups and downs of life together. Often words are said, and promises made. Rings are given, scarves are used to join the couple, hands are held, and agreements are signed, as part of the ceremony. For people who have a religious ceremony these customs are made sacred because they believe that their God is present to bless the marriage.

Choosing and finding a partner

The custom of choosing a person to marry varies in different cultures. Cultures are the ideas and ways of doing things in different societies. A society is made up of many people and groups.

In some groups, parents help their children to find a suitable partner. Lots of enquiries are made and when the right person is found the marriage is arranged. It is usual for Hindus, Muslims and Sikhs to have arranged marriages.

Some people try to find a partner with the help of a computer list. This help is organized by special firms called dating agencies. They try to match women and men who are looking for someone to marry. In other groups it is common for people to find their own partners by

Below Guests at a wedding procession in Sumatra are loaded with gifts which they will give to the bride and groom.

Tabira, a Muslim girl, describes a *mehndi* ceremony she went to: 'A few days before the man and lady are married there is a *mehndi* party. Everyone comes to the bride's house and the bride's hands and feet are painted with *mehndi* powder. Here the groom is being fed with sweets by the bride's family'

meeting people themselves. Whichever way people choose a partner, once they agree to get married, they are making an important decision to spend their lives with another person.

The wedding ceremony is a crossing-over time. Two people give up being single and cross over to become married. This means that there is a change of **status**. A woman becomes a wife, a man becomes a husband. Some women change their surname, and take on the name of their husband.

Inviting guests

Family and friends are invited to a wedding, usually by the parents of the bride. A wedding is a special and happy occasion, and guests enjoy taking part in the celebrations. They are **witnesses** at the wedding service, and often join in the wedding party afterwards.

The wedding ceremony is very personal to the couple. It marks the beginning of their life together. But it is also a public event, because a lot of people see that the bride and groom are leaving their families to start a new life together.

In most religious traditions, marriage customs are organized around four important aspects. When you read about the customs in this book you will find out which of these aspects they fit.

1. **Ritual** aspects. Rituals are actions that people do as part of a ceremony. Often these rituals carry a religious meaning. Some marriage rituals are performed by the couple, some by the guests, and some by the religious leader taking the ceremony. Christians have priests, vicars and ministers, Jews have a rabbi, Hindus have a priest and Muslims have an imam. Sikhs are married in front of a special book called the Guru Granth Sahib.

2. **Symbolic** aspects. A symbol can be an action or a thing that has a special meaning. There are many symbolic marriage customs to do with clothes worn, foods eaten and objects (such as rings) that are used in the wedding ceremony. Symbols often carry religious meanings.

3. **Social** aspects. Customs to do with the husband and wife living together. Social customs change from group to group. They depend on the background, culture and country that people come from.

4. **Legal** aspects. Customs to do with the marriage contract and with the promises made. Marriages have to be **registered** to be legal. Some couples will have a ceremony in a Registry Office and a religious ceremony. In some religious ceremonies the couple sign a special book called a register.

Above Signing the register at a Registry Office wedding makes the marriage legal.

Words and deeds

In religious ceremonies some of the customs are rituals, which are performed by the bride and groom and the leader taking the wedding service.

Promises, promises

Have you ever made a promise? Did you find it easy or hard to keep? How would you feel if someone broke a promise they made to you?

At many weddings you will hear couples making promises. Sometimes these promises are said out loud, sometimes the couple might sign a document, and sometimes both. The promises are important, so they are said or signed in the presence of the wedding guests. This shows that the couple intend to keep their promises so that

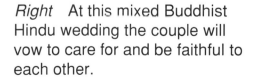
Right At this mixed Buddhist Hindu wedding the couple will vow to care for and be faithful to each other.

their marriage can work well. Some religious people believe that the promises are made in the presence of God. Although God is invisible (cannot be seen), people believe that He is still aware of the marriage and the promises made by the two people.

Above This Asian Muslim bride is reading her wedding contract. She will tell the witnesses three times that she agrees to the wedding.

Marriage as a sacrament

'Two into one doesn't go.' Is that what you have been taught? Christians turn this idea upside down! In marriage, it is believed that two people become one in a special way. They are joined together in the sight of God.

Right The Roman Catholic priest is giving wine to the bride during the wedding ceremony. She and her husband drink from the same cup. This shows that they will share their life, joys and sad times together.

Below After the rings have been blessed by the priest, the bride and groom exchange rings. Here the groom is placing the ring on the third finger of the bride's left hand.

The bride and groom make **vows** which join them together for life. It is also believed that God joins the couple together through the priest. The marriage is more than a human agreement. Because they make the promises through the priest, before God, the promises are special and holy. The couple have another partner to give them strength in their marriage. This is God. Roman Catholic and Orthodox Christians regard marriage as a sacrament.

Marriage vows

In many Christian weddings the bride and groom promise to love each other 'for better or worse, for richer or poorer, in sickness and in health' until they are parted by death. They each say these

11

words in front of the priest and loudly enough for the wedding guests to hear.

The bride and groom make their marriage vows when they give each other a ring. Each says:

'I give you this ring as a sign of our marriage
With my body I honour you
All that I am I give to you
All that I have I share with you
Within the love of God.'

While it is usual for women to wear wedding rings and to change their names, this has not always been the custom for men. Some people say that the custom of the bride's father 'giving away' his daughter is unfair because it treats men and women very differently. This custom used to show that women were the property of and needed the protection of men. Many women do not think so! Some brides today do not follow the custom of being given away by their fathers, and keep their own names.

Promises in a Hindu marriage are made before God, who is believed to be present in the form of a special fire. The wedding ceremony is led by a priest, or brahmin. The couple make their vows in the form of a custom called *Satapadi*, which means Seven Steps. These are taken as they walk around the sacred fire pot four times. These steps help the bride and groom to see that in their

Below A Hindu bride and groom stand in front of the sacred fire before they make the Seven Steps.

Above A Hindu bride places a garland of flowers over her husband's head. This custom acts as a sign to show that the couple will honour and respect each other.

marriage they will walk together and carry out seven duties. After the seventh step the bride and groom place their right hands on their partner's heart. They do not sign anything. They believe their signatures are written by their feet and with invisible ink on their hearts. The bride and groom agree that they will:

1. earn a living to provide food.

2. work for power and strength so that they can keep healthy and be strong for each other.

3. care for the **welfare** of each other so that their marriage can grow and prosper.

4. be concerned about each other's happiness and pleasure.

5. hope for children, who they will love and care for.

6. behave towards each other in an adaptable way and show that they can adjust to the other person, the place and the time.

7. work for close union and friendship so that they can live together as close friends.

By taking these steps they are making their vows.

At a Jewish wedding the groom says these words to the bride, as he puts a ring on her finger:

> *'By this you are* **consecrated** *to me according to the law of Moses and Israel.'*

The bride does not have to give or say anything to the groom. Accepting the ring is her way of showing that she agrees to marry him.

The meaning and duties of marriage

A Sikh wedding can be led by any Sikh woman or man who is well thought of in the community. Usually this is a person with a strong religious faith and knowledge. The ceremony is called *Anand Karaj*, which means 'ceremony of bliss', and takes place in front of the Sikh holy book, the Guru Granth Sahib. This shows that the couple are seeking the help, grace and blessing of God on their marriage. In a short talk the leader

Sujata, a Hindu girl describes her sister's wedding:
'The bride and groom both wore garlands made from flowers, and the bride had some beautiful jewellery. She wore special bracelets which our uncle gave her as a good luck present.
A bride can wear nine, eighteen or thirty-six bangles. My sister wore eighteen.'

explains the sacred meaning of marriage. Two hearts should become one, joined by the light of Sikh teachings in the Guru Granth Sahib.

Duties of husbands and wives are brought to the couple's attention. They are asked to be faithful and loyal to each other; to celebrate each other's joys and to be kind to one another in sorrow or pain. They are also asked to be kind, loving and respectful to their relatives. The couple show that they agree to the marriage when they bow before the Guru Granth Sahib.

Four marriage hymns called *Lavan* are read. Between each hymn musicians play, while the bride and groom walk clockwise around the Guru Granth Sahib. This shows that they accept each other and the duties of marriage. Sometimes the wedding guests throw bright flowers and petals at the couple

Right   At a Sikh wedding the couple are seated in front of the Guru Granth Sahib, the Sikh holy book.

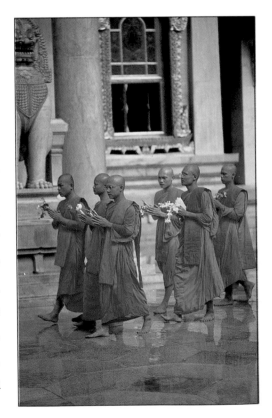

Left Joined together by a pink scarf, this Sikh bride and groom are walking clockwise around the Guru Granth Sahib to make their wedding vows.

as they walk around the Guru Granth Sahib for the fourth and last time.

Buddhists have a ceremony that is not considered sacred. However, the groom and bride make promises. They promise to be considerate to each other, to love, respect, and be faithful to one another. The man promises to provide gifts and presents to please his wife. The woman promises to be **hospitable** to her husband's family and friends. At the blessing of a Buddhist marriage by monks, the families promise to keep the five precepts (laws). These precepts teach people that the way to happiness is to live a good life by not killing, stealing, lying, or drinking alcohol. Men and women promise to be faithful to each other.

Buddhist monks and nuns live a life dedicated to the teachings of the Buddha and do not marry. Marriage is for **lay**

Above Buddhist monks do not marry. They live together in a community known as the *sangha.*

people; it is a social and not a religious occasion. Wedding customs vary according to the local community or culture.

Marriage contracts

At some weddings agreements are made, which help husbands and wives to be responsible to each other. These take note of the needs and the conditions that will create happiness for the couple.

The customs at Jewish wedding ceremonies depend on which branch of Judaism the bride and groom come from. Some will be **Orthodox** and some will be **Progressive** Jews.

Orthodox and some Progressive Jewish brides receive a *ketubah*, which is a marriage contract. It is a piece of paper like a certificate that is often beautifully decorated. The groom gives this to his

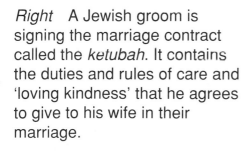

Right A Jewish groom is signing the marriage contract called the *ketubah*. It contains the duties and rules of care and 'loving kindness' that he agrees to give to his wife in their marriage.

bride before the marriage ceremony.

Traditionally the *ketubah* contains the duties and care that the husband agrees to give his wife. The husband is obliged to provide food, clothes and a home for his wife and children. The contract also contains rules that protect the wife and children in the event of death or divorce. A common practice today is that wives and husbands set out the terms of the agreement together. Once signed, the contract binds the couple together.

The Qur'an, the Muslim holy book, gives guidance on family life. It requires that a contract is made between the couple who are marrying. The contract is thought of as a human, not a sacred agreement. However, Muslims agree to live according to the teachings of Islam found in the Qur'an. The time when the contract is signed is called *Nikka*.

Muslims who come from Asia usually sign the marriage contract separately. The contract is taken by the imam to the groom, who signs it in the presence of four witnesses. Two witnesses must come from his family and two from the bride's family. Once the groom has signed, the contract is taken to the bride to sign. She says three times in front of the witnesses that she agrees to the marriage. The contract can be signed some time before the wedding ceremony, or on the same day.

Above The families of this Muslim couple have gone to a lot of trouble to make sure that they have chosen the right partners for their children. During the wedding ceremony the bride and groom agree to live together according to the teachings of their holy book, the Qur'an.

Signs and symbols

Symbols are actions or objects that represent or stand for something else. They often have a deep meaning. For example, the sacred fire at a Hindu wedding is a symbol of the presence of the Radiant One. Fire and light are symbols of God's wisdom, truth and justice. The fire at a Hindu wedding ceremony is the witness.

Right Four friends are holding a cloth on four poles over the bride and groom to make a chuppah. It is a canopy which they stand under when they make their promises to each other.

Many marriage customs include the use of signs and symbols. Jewish weddings take place under a canopy called a chuppah. This sometimes looks like a tent roof on four poles. It is a symbol of the new home the bride and groom will make. Often the chuppah poles are decorated with flowers and ribbons.

Cups or glasses

While a Jewish bride and groom stand under the chuppah, they drink from the same cup or glass of wine which has

Left The glass from which the bride and groom drink is stamped on and broken by the groom. Breaking and stamping on the glass is a sign that the wedding ceremony is completed. It reminds everyone present that love is fragile and that there will be happy and sad times.

Ezra, a pageboy at his teacher Miss Brown's wedding, says:
'In the synagogue I remember the rabbi blessed the wine. Eden drank it first, and then Miss Brown took some and Eden stamped on the glass. I shouted *Mazel Tov*, which means good luck and be happy, as loud as I could. I had to wear smart clothes and all the grown-ups made a fuss of me.'

been blessed. The ceremony ends with the breaking of the glass, which the groom stamps on. The broken glass is an important symbol. It suggests that love, like glass, is fragile, and therefore needs to be looked after. It also reminds Jewish people of the time in history when their temple in Jerusalem was destroyed.

Throwing food

Barley or grains are a symbol of the harvest and of fruitfulness. At some Jewish Orthodox weddings, grains are thrown at the bride, and a prayer is said which asks God to bless her and make her the mother of thousands. Rice is thrown at Hindu brides in the hope that they will have many children.

Wearing veils

Many Jewish and Christian brides get married in a veil which covers their face. It is a custom for some Orthodox Jewish brides to have a special ceremony just as they enter the synagogue. The groom lifts up the bride's veil to make sure that he is marrying the right woman!

This custom is carried out because of a story in the book of Genesis about Jacob and Rachel. Jacob worked for a man called Laban, and was in love with his daughter Rachel. He asked Laban if he could marry Rachel, but Laban tricked Jacob by giving him a veiled bride. She turned out to be Rachel's older sister Leah.

Wedding clothes

It is a custom for Jewish and Christian brides to wear a white or cream wedding dress. White is a symbol of purity. Jewish men wear a skull cap called a yarmulke and white **tallith** at their wedding. It is a custom for men to be buried in a tallith, so this is both a symbol of joy and mourning.

Below The groom is lifting the veil to make sure he has the right bride. He does not want to end up like Jacob and marry the wrong one!

Right This Hindu bride from Nepal is wearing the traditional red sari embroidered with gold threads, and beautiful gold jewellery.

Asian brides, whether Hindu, Muslim or Sikh, usually get married in red or a deep pink-coloured silk, embroidered with gold threads. Red is considered to be a happy, bright colour, appropriate for the wedding, which is an occasion of excitement and joy. Hindu brides wear a sari, and a long scarf to cover the head called a *chunni*. It is usual for Muslim and Sikh brides to wear special clothes called *shalwar* and *kameez*, with a long scarf called a *dupatta*. A *kameez* is a long, elegant and beautifully embroidered

23

tunic, worn over loose or baggy trousers called *shalwar*.

Asian men get married in their own traditional dress, a Punjabi suit or a western suit. Often a long white jacket with a stand-up collar is worn over white trousers. Sikhs wear **turbans**, often a deep red colour, while Hindu men sometimes wear a special hat called a *tupi*, or a turban made to look like a crown, decorated with a feather, sequins or jewels.

Left Behind his *kalgri*, or face mask, the Sikh bridegroom has a dark red turban. He is also wearing a pink scarf which will be used as a symbol to join him and the bride.

Above Bridesmaids and pageboys dress up to follow the bride on her wedding day.

Bridesmaids and pageboys

Although you will see bridesmaids and pageboys who attend the bride at many weddings, this custom is not religious. But it shows that the bride is special, like a queen on her wedding day.

Rings

Have you ever wondered why wedding rings are so plain? Usually they are smooth gold bands that have no beginning and no end. Rings are like circles of love that have no beginning and no end, so they are thought of as symbols of **eternity**. They show that the couple belong together and hope to stay with each other for life.

After the blessing at a Jewish wedding, the groom places a plain wedding ring on the index (first) finger of the bride's right hand. The custom requires that

Right Wedding rings are worn by the bride and groom to show that they will give their love to each other for ever. The Christian custom of placing wedding rings on the third finger of the left hand grew from the belief that the third finger has a direct vein to the heart.

something valuable should be given to the bride. Some people give the bride a gold coin. It is not necessary to give a ring, but it is usual. Whatever is given is placed on the bride's right hand. Two witnesses must be present. Placing the ring on the right index finger makes it easier for the witnesses to see.

Painting patterns on hands and feet

At many Asian weddings, whether Hindu, Muslim or Sikh, you will see that the bride has beautiful patterns painted on her hands and the soles of her feet. This is a social and not a religious custom. The patterns are painted with a powder made from the crushed leaves of the *mehndi* tree, which turns the skin a warm red colour.

Left This Muslim bride's hands are decorated with *mehndi* patterns for her wedding day.

The custom of painting the hairline or parting red in Hindu weddings is often done by the groom after the couple have taken the Seven Steps. It is a sign that the woman is married and that she belongs to her husband and his family.

Above Having a special meal after the ceremony is a traditional marriage custom. Delicious food is served to the wedding guests at this reception in Pakistan.

Special food

At most wedding parties there is special food. For Christians in Britain it is a custom to finish off the meal with a wedding cake. The cake is usually made of fruit, covered with white icing, and has three tiers or levels. Traditionally, the couple are expected to save one level of their wedding cake to celebrate the birth of their first child.

After the ceremony

After some Hindu wedding ceremonies, there is a custom that the bride and groom go home, eat, and play what is called 'the ring game'. The priest puts a ring in a tank of red-coloured water with rice and stones in it. The bride and groom have to find the ring three or more times. The person who finds it most is said to be the ruler of the house!

There is also the custom that the bride is **ransomed** by her sisters. The bride-groom has to give rings or presents to the sisters of the bride before he can take her to his family.

At a Greek Orthodox Christian wedding party there is music, and the bride and groom often dance with a white scarf between them.

When a couple finally leave after all the wedding celebrations, they begin their new life together. Brides in all traditions leave in a new set of clothes. Sometimes her parents buy these for her. A Hindu bride leaves the wedding in special clothes bought for her by her husband's family.

Sikh weddings often end with a farewell ceremony called *Doli*. The mother and sisters of the bride dress her in new clothes and jewellery and say

Alexis went to an Orthodox Christian wedding:
'At the very end they pin a lot of money on to the couple's clothes for their honeymoon - it's got to be a note £5 or over. People give what they can, but often £20 and £50 notes are pinned on the bride's dress. Anyway, they get a lot of money.'

goodbye. She is taken away in a brightly decorated car by the bridegroom to his family home.

One custom that sometimes takes place after a Christian wedding is 'crossing the threshold'. The man carries his bride over the threshold or doorway of their new home. Doors are important symbols. When a couple 'cross the threshold' they are opening the door to their new life together.

Married life often begins with a holiday or a honeymoon. This is a time when the newlyweds can get to know each other better and make plans for their future together.

Below Together and alone at last! Newlyweds leave on a ferry which begins their journey to their secret honeymoon.

Glossary

Ceremony   A formal act, often carried out as part of a custom.
Consecrated   Dedicated to something or someone in particular.
Eternity   Endless time.
Hospitable   Welcoming to visitors.
Lay people   People who are not religious leaders.
Legal   To do with the law.
Orthodox Christians   Members of the division of the Christian church mainly based in Eastern Europe.
Orthodox Jews   Jews who strictly follow the teachings God revealed to the prophet, Moses.
Progressive Jews   Jews who believe that the teachings of Moses can be adapted for the modern world.
Ransomed   Held as a prisoner until money is paid for a person's release.
Registered   Written down or recorded in a special book.
Ritual   To do with carrying out religious services in a set way.

Sacrament   Something that is believed to have a special religious significance. Christians who are Roman Catholic and Greek Orthodox regard marriage as a sacrament.
Sacred   Holy, relating to God.
Sari   Traditional dress of women in India, Pakistan and surrounding countries. It is a long, narrow piece of cloth wrapped around the body.
Social   To do with people and society.
Status   A person's position in society.
Symbolic   Standing for something else.
Tallith   A white prayer shawl worn by Jewish men.
Turban   A man's head-dress, which is a long length of cloth wrapped around the head.
Uldi   An orange paste used by people in Bengal.
Vows   Solemn promises.
Welfare   Well-being.
Witnesses   People who see an event happen.

Further information

Books to read

The following books will help you find out more about marriage customs:
Wedding by Lynne Harrigan (A & C Black, 1991)
Marriage Customs by Jon Mayled (Wayland, 1986)

These series also contain useful information about the religions dealt with in this book:
My Belief (Franklin Watts, 1989)
Our Culture (Franklin Watts, 1989)
Religions of the World (Simon & Schuster, 1992)
Religions of the World (Wayland, 1986)

Picture acknowledgements

The publishers wish to thank the following for supplying the photographs in this book:
Cephas Picture Library 11 (top, Frank B Higham, bottom, Mick Rock), 28 (Helen Stylianou); Chapel Studios 5 (Zul Mukhida); Eye Ubiquitous 6 (left, P M Field), 8, 12 (Helene Rogers), 13 (Helene Rogers); Hutchison Library cover, 10 (Christine Pemberton), 20 (Liba Taylor), 22 (Liba Taylor), 24, 29 (Robert Francis); Ann & Bury Peerless 15, 16 (top); Tony Stone Worldwide 16 (Hilarie Kavanagh), 23 (David Hanson); Wayland Picture Library 4, 18, 26, 27; ZEFA 14, 17, 19, 25 (both).

Index

Numbers in **bold** indicate photographs